ENCOUNTERS WITH THE PAST

MEET THE
TUDORS

Alex Woolf

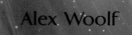
Gareth Stevens
PUBLISHING

Please visit our website, **www.garethstevens.com**. For a free color catalog of all our high-quality books, call toll free 1-800-542-2595 or fax 1-877-542-2596.

Woolf, Alex.
Meet the Tudors / by Alex Woolf.
p. cm. — (Encounters with the past)
Includes index.
ISBN 978-1-4824-0898-0 (pbk.)
ISBN 978-1-4824-0899-7 (6-pack)
ISBN 978-1-4824-0897-3 (library binding)
1. Great Britain — History — Tudors, 1485-1603 — Juvenile literature.
I. Woolf, Alex, 1964- II. Title.
DA316.W66 2015
942.05—d23

First Edition

Published in 2015 by
Gareth Stevens Publishing
111 East 14th Street, Suite 349
New York, NY 10003

Editors: Joe Harris and Nicola Barber
Design: Elaine Wilkinson
Cover design: Elaine Wilkinson

Cover pictures Shutterstock:Shutterstock: Little Moreton Hall Shelli Jensen, Elizabethan lady Lucy, coins Sponner, lute Nahariyani.

Picture acknowledgements: Alamy: p6 John Wheeler; p12 Andrew Michael; p15 bottom Image Asset Management Ltd.; p18 Neil Setchfield; p24 Adrian Buck; p26 Image Asset Management Ltd. The Bridgeman Art Library: p11 top Bonhams, London, UK; p13 top The Stapleton Collection; p27 top Private Collection. Corbis: p13 bottom Robert Harding World Imagery; p22 Lebrecht Music & Arts. Getty: pp24-5 VisitBritain/Grant Pritchard. Guarderobe (www.guarderobe.co.uk): p20, p21 top. Renaissance Footnotes (www.basdance.hampshire.org.uk): pp4 inset top and 19 bottom Richard Carter. Shutterstock: title page young woman Jeff Banke; p4 background Khunaspix, Tudor rose Sana Design, coins Sponner, wallet Kostenko Maxim; pp5, 10-11 and 28 1000 Words; pp6-7 Aleksandra Nadeina; p7 top Debu55y; p7 bottom Anderl; pp8-9 Benson HE; p8 Darja Vorontsova; p9 top and bottom Peter Lorimer; p10 Raulin; p11 bottom Kiselev Andrey Valerevich; pp12-13 Manuel Alvarez; pp14-15 David Hughes; p14 Sergey Kamshylin; p15 top Boykov; pp16-17 and contents Padmayogini; p16 and title page Igor Bulgarin; p17 top Kamira; p17 bottom Lance Bellers; pp18-19 Pitamaha; p19 top Boykov; pp20-21 Gts; p21 bottom Ermess; pp22-3 Tom Gowanlock; p23 top Clearimages; p25 top Rob Hainer; p25 bottom Hein Nouwens; pp26-7 and title page David Fowler; p27 bottom Marbury; p28 AdStock RF; p29 Shelli Jensen. Wikimedia Commons: p23 bottom Dcoetzee.

Printed in the United States of America

CPSIA compliance information: Batch CS15GS: For further information contact Gareth Stevens, New York, New York at 1-800-542-2595.

Contents

Into the Past 4

The Duchess's Necklace 6

Talking to the Kitchen Maid 8

The Hardworking Laundry Maid 10

In the Library 12

The Young Archer 14

Meeting the Actor 16

A Chat with the Musician 18

At the Barber-Surgeon's House 20

A Visit to the Priest 22

Finding the Soldier 24

The Justice of the Peace 26

Back to the Present 28

Glossary 30

For More Information 31

Index 32

Into the Past

You're on a family vacation to England. Your family's visit to the old Tudor house museum is nearly over. It's time to meet the rest of your family in the gift shop. You quicken your pace along the creaking hallway. You got sidetracked and now you're not sure exactly where you are!

Suddenly, right in front of you, a door appears. There are no walls around it – it's just a plain, wooden door in the middle of the hallway. For a moment, you stand amazed. Then you open the door and find yourself in a small room with a stone floor. On a table in the middle of the room is a pile of clothing, a leather pouch containing coins, and a parchment with these words written on it:

Your Mission

You are going back to the year 1585 CE, when Queen Elizabeth I was on the throne. Your mission is to meet people and find out about their lives. The mission will last six hours.

▲ The first Tudor king, Henry VII, used this double rose as the emblem of England because it combined the red rose of the House of Lancaster and the white rose of the House of York. Henry (a Lancastrian) defeated Richard III (a Yorkist) at the Battle of Bosworth in 1485.

At that moment, another door in the wall in front of you starts to open. On the table are a woolen dress, a pair of breeches, a doublet, a feathered hat, and a linen cap. You choose an outfit and secure the money pouch to your belt. Then you take a deep breath, and walk through the door.

The Duchess's Necklace

The house looks much the same as before, but it is now bustling with activity, with servants coming and going. You sense from their faces that something is wrong. The lady of the house appears. She looks very upset. She tells you that her favorite necklace has gone missing – it may have been stolen. You offer to help find it, but you ask whether she would mind answering some questions first.

WHAT DO YOU DO ALL DAY?

I am in charge of the household while my husband, the duke, is away at court. Much of my time is taken up with supervising the servants. In my leisure time, I enjoy riding, hunting with dogs or falcons, playing cards, or doing needlework. Today, however, is my birthday, and I'm looking forward to an afternoon of being entertained by actors and musicians.

HOW DID YOU MEET YOUR HUSBAND?

Our marriage was arranged. My father chose my husband because, like me, he comes from a wealthy family. I met my husband for the first time on our wedding day. I was 14 years old. Luckily, I have come to love him. If I didn't, it would be sad, because I have no power to divorce him.

HOW MANY CHILDREN DO YOU HAVE?

I have three – two boys and a girl. I have had five children altogether, but two died as infants. I am very fortunate to have survived five pregnancies – many women don't – and to have produced two healthy sons to continue the family line. I don't see much of my children because the servants look after them most of the time.

Talking to the Kitchen Maid

The duchess has summoned the parish constable to the house. He is in charge of law and order in the village. The duchess believes a servant may have stolen the necklace, so the constable goes downstairs to the kitchens to find out more, and you follow. While the constable questions the servants, you sit with one of the kitchen maids and ask her some questions of your own.

WHAT IS LIFE LIKE AS A SERVANT?

The hours are very long, and I spend most of my life here in the kitchen. I'm given clothing, food, and a bed in the attic with the other maids. I'm allowed a little bit of time off to pray, and to attend church on Sundays. If I'm disobedient, I'm punished with a fine.

WHAT SORT OF FOOD DO YOU PREPARE?

Some of the meals are enormous! If the family has guests, we often prepare at least 12 different courses. A typical meal could include roast meat, followed by several different kinds of poultry, then pies, salads, and vegetables. After that come the sweet courses: tarts, creamy syllabubs, fruit, and nuts.

WHAT DO PEOPLE DRINK?

The water here is not very clean, so at mealtimes everyone drinks beer or cider – even the children. We brew our own beer and cider here, as do most households. If you go the tavern, you can buy wine, a kind of sherry called sack, and a cider made from pears, known as perry. But my favorite is mead – I like the taste of the honey and spices.

This type of leather tankard was made for use on ships in Tudor times, as it did not fall over easily.

9

The Hardworking Laundry Maid

N one of the servants in the kitchens knows anything about the necklace. You follow the constable as he goes out of the door and heads down to a stream that runs through the grounds. The laundry maid is working there. She answers the constable's questions while continuing to beat the dirt out of some clothing with a heavy wooden bat. Afterwards, you have a few words with her.

WHAT IS YOUR JOB?

I wash all the clothes and linen by hand, which involves a lot of soaking, scrubbing, and beating. I use soap made from animal fat and a liquid called lye, made from rainwater and the ashes from the fire. I usually dry the laundry by hanging it over hedges in the sun, but this can be risky as the clothes are sometimes stolen by thieves.

WHAT SORT OF CLOTHES DO WEALTHY WOMEN WEAR?

Ladies wear ankle-length dresses of silk or velvet covered with rich embroidery. These days, the fashion is for a narrow waist and a wide skirt. So ladies wear an underskirt with whalebone hoops sewn into it, known as a Spanish farthingale. The hoops increase in size from waist to ground to make a bell-shaped cage.

A portrait of a wealthy lady wearing a dress with a lace ruff, a narrow waist, and a full skirt.

WHAT DO MEN WEAR?

Gentlemen wear a linen shirt underneath an embroidered doublet, which is a short, close-fitting padded jacket. Sleeves can be either close-fitting or wide and padded. On their legs, they wear short pants and hose. They wear fancy shoes with high heels, and frilly lace ruffs, stiffened with starch, around their necks.

In the Library

The laundry maid tells the constable that the children of the house sometimes steal things. The constable asks you to help him look for them. After a quick search, you find the younger boy in the library, being taught by his tutor. The boy is using a quill pen to copy out a religious text written on a hornbook. While the constable questions the boy, you talk to the tutor.

DO YOU TEACH ALL THE CHILDREN?

No! I only teach the two boys. I think academic education is a waste of time for girls, even for those from wealthy families. Girls are taught practical subjects, such as sewing, embroidery, and cooking, which will be useful for running a home after they're married. They may also learn dancing, music, archery, and riding.

WHAT DO YOU TEACH THE BOYS?

I teach them spelling, reading, writing, and counting. The younger boy is nine years old. When he's 11, he will start to learn Latin, English grammar, history, and to study the Bible. He will also receive training in dance, music, drawing, debating, and making speeches.

A tutor teaches a child with the help of a hornbook – a flat piece of wood with letters and numbers written on it, held by a handle.

DO ALL CHILDREN HAVE TUTORS?

Only the richest families can afford to pay tutors to teach their children. Most poor children get no education at all. Wealthier families send their boys to petty school, then to a grammar school when they are 11 years old. Grammar school boys spend an average of nine hours a day at school, six days a week!

This is the schoolroom in Stratford-upon-Avon where William Shakespeare was educated.

The Young Archer

You go with the constable in search of the elder brother. You find him practicing archery in the garden. He is using a longbow made of yew, with three strings of hemp. After the constable has finished asking him questions, you engage him in conversation.

WHY ARE YOU PRACTICING ARCHERY?

Because I enjoy it, and because it is an important part of my education. In this country, all fit men over the age of 24 should be able to shoot a target a good distance away. That's the law. I'm 15 now, so I need to keep practicing. As well as a longbow like this one, I also use a crossbow.

WHAT OTHER SPORTS AND GAMES DO YOU ENJOY?

We often go hunting and hawking, and sometimes take part in jousting tournaments. I also like playing real tennis, cards, dice, bowls, and skittles. Occasionally, for a treat, we go to the bear-gardens and watch some bear-baiting. We like to see a good fight between the dogs and the bear. It's a very popular pastime in this country.

Hunting with hawks and falcons was popular in Tudor times.

DO POOR PEOPLE PLAY SPORTS?

It's not encouraged. Poor people are supposed to save their energy for work. My father says that in the time of King Henry VIII, the poor used to play soccer. But it was banned because so many people were being injured. It's a very violent game!

A Tudor game of soccer. The leather ball was often stuffed with animal hair.

Meeting the Actor

The elder son is innocent of the theft, but he suggests you question the touring players who have come to the house in honor of the duchess's birthday. The actors are busy setting up their stage in another part of the grounds. The constable is very suspicious of the traveling players – he thinks they are all scoundrels! While he questions their manager, you chat with one of the actors.

WHY ARE YOU PERFORMING HERE?

Our company has a permanent theater in London. But during the summer months, the city is a dangerous place to be because there are often outbreaks of the plague. So we tour the countryside, setting up temporary stages in inn-yards, or in the grounds of big houses like this one. Touring is hard work, as we have to carry all the costumes and props around with us.

WHAT IS YOUR THEATER LIKE?

My friend William Shakespeare describes it as a "wooden O." It's a large, round timber building with an open space in the middle surrounded by galleries of seats. The roof over the galleries is thatched. The stage is built out into the central space. Behind the stage is a building that contains the dressing rooms.

The Globe Theatre in London was built in 1599 by Shakespeare's company of actors, the Lord Chamberlain's Men. This is a modern reconstruction of the original theater.

WHAT'S IT LIKE BEING AN ACTOR?

Like the constable, the authorities treat us with suspicion, but we're respectable enough folk! There are no acting schools, so we learn our craft on stage in front of an audience. Women aren't allowed to perform, so we use boys to play the parts of women in the plays. Some of my friends have become quite famous, like the tragic actor Richard Burbage, and the comic Richard Tarleton.

A Chat with the Musician

Despite the constable's suspicions, the necklace isn't found among the actors. But they are not the only visitors to the house. As part of the duchess's birthday celebrations, some musicians have also been invited to perform, and it is time for the constable to question them. When he's finished, you ask one of the musicians about Tudor entertainment.

WHAT ARE THE MOST POPULAR ENTERTAINMENTS?

We're often asked to play lute music, or to sing songs called madrigals. Wealthy people sometimes employ us to perform masques. These are short plays in verse with dances and music. They are performed in costume with very elaborate scenery. Historical pageants are popular, as well as tournaments with armored knights jousting on horseback.

WHAT ENTERTAINMENTS DOES THE QUEEN ENJOY?

At the royal palaces, there is a permanent staff of musicians, jesters, storytellers, jugglers, acrobats, and even performing animals. Queen Elizabeth loves to dance, and especially favors firework displays.
I have heard that when King Henry VIII was married to his second wife, Anne Boleyn, they were both keen gamblers. They made card playing and dice games popular.

Jousting was a popular sport in Tudor times.

WHAT OTHER ENTERTAINMENTS DO PEOPLE LIKE?

Both wealthy and poor people love dancing. Courtly dances are very refined. Ordinary people enjoy lively jigs and reels to the accompaniment of pipes and drums. And they catch up on the news when the ballad singers visit their village. These singers travel from place to place with lively songs about murders and other sensational events.

At the Barber-Surgeon's House

The musicians do not have the necklace. But back at the house, one of the servants has found a clue: a broken window and beneath it, a pool of blood. Perhaps the thief was injured as he made his escape? The constable decides to visit the local barber-surgeon to ask if he has treated anyone recently. You accompany the constable to the house and take the opportunity to ask the barber-surgeon about his life.

WHAT'S A TYPICAL DAY FOR YOU?

I deal with all sorts of everyday accidents and illnesses. I set broken bones and treat wounds. Bloodletting is a good treatment for many illnesses – I believe that it's important to get rid of bad blood to help restore the body to health. I make a small cut in the patient's arm to let the blood flow out, or sometimes I apply leeches to the skin and they suck out the bad blood. I also offer haircuts and shaves, and pull out rotten teeth.

SO HOW ARE YOU DIFFERENT FROM A PHYSICIAN?

Physicians have a higher status than barber-surgeons. They go to university and often do many years of study at medical school, usually in France or Italy. But unlike us barber-surgeons, physicians don't do much hands-on work! They listen to patients describe their symptoms, and they often examine their urine. Then they decide what's wrong with the help of textbooks.

A physician at his work table.

WHAT ABOUT PEOPLE WHO CAN'T AFFORD A PHYSICIAN?

Most ordinary people never go to a physician. In most families, knowledge of traditional remedies gets passed down from mother to daughter. Most sick people are treated at home. People often seek advice from an apothecary – there's one in most villages. Many apothecaries offer free advice, then make their living by selling herbal medicines.

An apothecary's supplies.

A Visit to the Priest

The barber-surgeon tells the constable that the parish priest came in earlier today with an injury, so you go to the local church to see if he might be the culprit. The priest has a freshly bandaged leg wound. After the constable has talked to him, you question him about religion in Tudor times.

WHAT KIND OF CHRISTIANITY DO YOU PRACTICE?

Today, under Queen Elizabeth, we worship as Protestants. But there has been a great deal of religious upheaval over the past 40 years. This country was Roman Catholic until Henry VIII made himself Supreme Head of a new Church of England. During the reign of Henry's eldest daughter, Mary I, we turned back to the Roman Catholic Church again. It was a time of great terror and turmoil, when many Protestants were burned at the stake because they would not accept the Roman Catholic faith.

The leading Protestants, Hugh Latimer, Nicholas Ridley, and Thomas Cranmer were all burned at the stake in the reign of Mary I.

WHAT DID ELIZABETH I DO?

When Elizabeth came to the throne in 1558, she wanted to settle the religious question once and for all. She restored the Protestant faith, but she tried to please the Catholics as well. She allowed some things from the Catholic Church to remain, so unlike other Protestant countries, we still have bishops and our priests wear special clothes called vestments during services. Elizabeth produced a prayer book in English – but she also allowed a Latin version to be printed.

SO ARE CATHOLICS ALLOWED TO WORSHIP?

This is now a Protestant country, but some Catholics, known as recusants, continue to worship in secret. A few would like to make England a Catholic country once again by bringing Elizabeth's cousin, Mary Queen of Scots, to the throne. These plotters are dangerous people! Elizabeth deals with them harshly. Any who are caught are put to death.

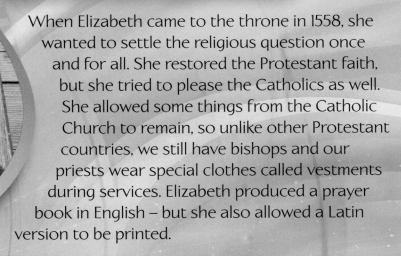

As a Roman Catholic, Mary Queen of Scots was a constant threat to her cousin, Elizabeth I. Eventually Elizabeth ordered Mary's execution, in 1586.

Finding the Soldier

The priest explains that, earlier in the day, a soldier with an injured arm ran into the church and told the priest to hide the stolen necklace. When the priest refused, there was a struggle. The priest was wounded, and the soldier fled. He took the necklace with him. The constable knows where the local soldiers live. As he starts his inquiries, you decide to find out about a soldier's life.

ARE YOU IN AN ARMY?

No, England doesn't have a professional army. Instead there are groups called trained bands. All men who own property, and their grown-up sons, must join their local trained band – although many send their servants to training sessions instead. The sessions are held once a month during the summer, and we get paid a shilling a day. We get to keep our armor.

WHAT WEAPONS DO YOU FIGHT WITH?

Foot soldiers fight with heavy broadswords, battleaxes, and pikes. We also use the halberd, a double-bladed axe on a long pole with a spear point at the top. The billhook is good for attacking knights on horseback, and the mace is effective against armor. We also have firearms like the arquebus and the caliver. Occasionally we might get to use a musket.

WHAT HAPPENS IN A BATTLE?

The usual tactics are to try to weaken the enemy by bombarding them with arrows, and shots from the arquebus and calivers. This is followed up by a charge. We use our archers to shoot at close range into the flanks of the enemy. The foot soldiers fight with their pikes and axes, halberds and swords, in an attempt to crush the enemy by brute force.

A soldier equipped with an arquebus – a type of firearm popular in Tudor times.

The Justice of the Peace

While you have been talking to the soldier, the constable has found the thief. The necklace is returned to the duchess, and the culprit is taken before the Justice of the Peace. As it's the soldier's first offense, he escapes having his hand cut off. Instead his punishment is to be branded with the letter "F" for felon. After the sentence has been passed, you talk to the judge.

WHAT HAPPENS IF YOU'RE ACCUSED OF A CRIME?

You have to appear in court, or else risk losing your house and possessions. Every man is expected to know enough about the law to defend himself in court, but wealthy people usually pay a lawyer to defend them. However, lawyers have quite a bad name. Most people believe they make a living out of other people's misery.

Judges in their robes during the time of Elizabeth I.

WHAT KIND OF CRIMINALS DO YOU DEAL WITH?

Petty criminals mainly – beggars, vagrants, thieves, nippers (they cut purses off people's belts), footpads (robbers on foot), highwaymen, pickpockets, swindlers, and priggers of prancers (horse thieves). More serious crimes such as murder or treason are tried at a different court.

A beggar is ignored by a rich man. Begging was often severely punished.

HOW ARE CRIMINALS PUNISHED?

Beggars, vagrants, and drunks are put in the stocks or the pillory, then tied to the back of a cart and rushed out of town. For more serious crimes, the punishment is usually hanging. We have prisons, but we don't use them for punishment. People are put in prison to wait for their trial, or until their punishment is carried out.

The stocks had holes for a person's head and arms (or legs) to be locked in place. People were often left in the stocks for days at a time.

Back to the Present

Your six hours are over. You run back to the house, past the duchess's birthday celebrations, and into the hallway where you first arrived. There is a bright flash of light and the doorway reappears. You pass through it into the little room where you leave your Tudor garments and change back into your own clothes. Then you go through another door and find yourself outside the Tudor house's gift shop. You rejoin your family.

WHAT WAS THE LEGACY OF THE TUDORS?

It was during the Tudor period that England transformed from a Roman Catholic into a Protestant country. The Tudors also left their mark on our historic towns and cities, with their distinctive black-and-white half-timbered buildings. And around the time of your visit, the actor William Shakespeare began writing the plays that are today regarded by many as the finest ever written in the English language.

SHAKSPERE

Little Moreton Hall is a half-timbered building that dates from the 1500s.

WHAT ABOUT TUDOR JUSTICE?

You spent much of your six hours with the parish constable, but you didn't manage to question him! You decide to find out more about Tudor justice. You discover that the Tudors didn't have a police force. Instead a group of armed citizens, called the watch, kept law and order in each parish. The parish constable was in charge of the watch. Many crimes were committed because people were desperately poor. And punishments were often extremely harsh –people were beaten for begging and often hanged for theft.

Glossary

apothecary A person who made up and sold remedies from herbs and other ingredients.

arquebus An early type of gun, rather like a rifle, with a long barrel.

bear-baiting A form of cruel entertainment in which dogs were set upon a captive bear.

bear-garden An arena with a circular high fenced area (the pit) and raised seating for spectators, where bear-baiting or other animal fights took place.

billhook A weapon made from a pole with a hooked blade mounted below a spearhead, with spikes added to the back of the blade. It was used by foot soldiers against armored cavalry.

caliver An improved version of the arquebus, introduced in the early 1500s.

falcon A bird of prey often used for hunting.

hawking The sport of hunting with a trained hawk.

hemp Fiber extracted from the stem of the hemp plant, used to make string, rope, fabric, and paper.

hornbook A wooden tablet protected by a thin plate of horn that was used to teach letters, numbers and the Lord's Prayer.

hose Men's tight-fitting trousers.

inn-yard The courtyard of an inn, where plays were often performed.

joust A sporting contest in which two armored opponents on horseback fight with lances, trying to knock each other off.

leech A type of worm that feeds by sucking blood from a host, such as a human.

lute A stringed musical instrument with a long neck, a rounded body, and a flat front that is played by plucking the strings.

lye A liquid consisting mainly of potassium carbonate (potash) that was historically made from rainwater and ashes.

mace A heavy club, usually with a metal head and spikes.

madrigal A song for several voices, usually sung without instrumental accompaniment.

mead A type of alcoholic drink produced from honey, spices, and water.

musket A gun with a long barrel, usually fired from the shoulder. It was heavier and more powerful than the arquebus or caliver.

pageant An outdoor performance of a historical scene.

petty school A school in the Elizabethan era for boys between five and 11 years old.

pillory A wooden framework with holes for the head and hands in which an offender was imprisoned and exposed to public abuse.

plague A deadly infectious disease that is spread to humans by the fleas on rats.

real tennis An early form of tennis, played with a solid ball on an enclosed court.

reel A lively folk dance.

syllabub A whipped cream dessert.

tournament A sporting event in which knights jousted on horseback, the winner receiving a prize.

vagrant A homeless person who lives by begging.

vestments Robes worn by a clergyman during services.

For More Information

WEBSITES

www.bbc.co.uk/history/british/tudors/
This BBC site contains sections on the Tudor monarchs, Shakespeare, daily life, exploration, art, and architecture.

www.henryviiiandthetudors.co.uk
A website focusing on Henry VIII, but which contains some interesting facts about Tudor life in general.

www.historyonthenet.com/Tudors/tudorsmain.htm
A website devoted to the Tudors, with sections on monarchs, famous events, society, food, costume, entertainment, and much else.

www.superbrainybeans.co.uk/history/videos/terrible-tudors.html
A site containing video clips from the 'Terrible Tudors' segments of the Horrible Histories TV series – a humorous, yet factual take on the history of the period.

www.tudorbritain.org
A site that examines real documents and objects from Tudor times. It includes sections on court life, daily life, entertainment, religion, and trade.

BOOKS

Entertainment (Tudor Life) by Nicola Barber (Wayland, 2013)
Everyday Life (Discover the Tudors) by Moira Butterfield (Franklin Watts, 2013)
Tudor Britain (History on Your Doorstep) by Stewart Ross (Franklin Watts, 2012)
The Tudors (Hail!) by Philip Steele (Wayland, 2013)
The Tudors (History from Objects) by Angela Royston (Wayland, 2012)

Index

acrobats 19
actors 6, 16-17, 18
apothecaries 21
archery 12, 14-15, 25
army 24
arquebus 25

ballad singers 19
barber-surgeon 20-21, 22
battleaxes 25
Battle of Bosworth 4
bear-baiting 15
beer 9
beggars 27, 29
billhooks 25
bloodletting 20
Boleyn, Anne 19
bowls 15
broadswords 25
Burbage, Richard 17

calivers 25
cards 15, 19
children 7, 12-13, 14-15
Church of England 22
cider 9
clothes 4, 5, 8, 10-11, 28
companies of actors 16, 17
Cranmer, Thomas 22
crimes 10, 27, 29
criminals 26-27, 29
crossbows 14

dancing 12, 13, 18, 19
dice 15, 19

doublets 11
drinking water 9
duchess 6-7, 8, 26, 28

education 12-13
    for boys 12-13, 14
    for girls 12
Elizabeth I, Queen 4, 19, 22, 23, 26

falcons 6, 15
fireworks 19
food 8, 9
foot soldiers 25

Globe Theatre 17
grammar schools 13

halberds 25
hanging 27, 29
hawking 15
Henry VII, King 4
Henry VIII, King 15, 19, 22
hornbooks 12, 13
hunting 6, 15

illnesses 20-21

jesters 19
jousting tournaments 15, 18, 19
jugglers 19
Justice of the Peace 26-7

kitchen maid 8-9
kitchens 8-9

Latimer, Hugh 22
laundry 10
laundry maid 10-11, 12

law and order 26-7, 29
lawyers 26
leeches 20
longbows 14
Lord Chamberlain's Men 17
lutes 18

madrigals 18
marriage 7
Mary I, Queen 22
Mary Queen of Scots 23
masques 18
mead 9
medicines 21
musicians 6, 18-19, 20
musket 25

needlework 6, 12

pageants 18
parish constable 8, 10, 12, 14, 16, 17, 18, 20, 22, 24, 26, 29
perry (cider) 9
petty schools 13
physicians 21
pikes 25
pillory 27
plague 16
prayer books 23
priest 22-23, 24
prisons 27
Protestants 22, 23, 28
punishments 8, 22, 23, 26-7, 29

real tennis 15
recusants 23
religion 22-23
Richard III, King 4
Ridley, Nicholas 22
Roman Catholic Church 22, 23, 28
ruffs 11

sack (sherry) 9
servants 6, 7, 8-9, 10-11, 20
Shakespeare, William 13, 17, 28
ships 9
skittles 15
soap 10
soldier 24-25, 26
Spanish farthingales 11
stocks 27
storytellers 19

tankards 9
Tarleton, Richard 17
theaters 16, 17
thieves 27, 29
trained bands 24
Tudor rose 4
tutor 12-13

urine 21

vagrants 27
vestments 23

watch, the 29
weapons 24-5
wine 9